MW01126249

The Break Up

The Break Up

The Break Up

The Break Up

Breaking Up with Sin and Breaking into Spiritual Freedom

By Sylvester Sumler Jr.

Copyright Page

ISBN: 978-0-57867456-8 (Paperback)

First Paperback Printed & Published 4/2020
Sylvester L. Sumler Jr.., Norfolk, VA
www.slsumler.com

Production Affiliates…
Editor – Charmaine Williams, MSW & Sharonja Houston
Illustrator – Jason Josiah, Living Word Illustrations
Contribution - Write It Out Publishing LLC

All scripture quotations are taken from the Holy Bible, all versions.

Sumler Ministries

Norfolk, VA

Dedication

This book is dedicated to every person who is experiencing bondage in their life. To every person battling addictions, and to every struggling Christian pursuing wholeness in Christ.

Acknowledgements

I would like to take the time to recognize my family who has been a strong support system through every season of my life and in ministry. To Sonya Sumler (mother), Sylvester Sumler Sr. (father), Trae'Vis Sumler (brother), Priscilla Taylor (grandmother), Ros Hall (Godmother), Angela Dance (aunt), and to my beautiful fiance, Charmaine Williams.

Table of Contents

DEDICATION .... **III**

ACKNOWLEDGEMENTS .... **V**

SIX REASONS IT'S HARD TO BREAK UP **2**

CHAPTER ONE

I DON'T WANT TO LIVE LIKE THIS

THE CONVICTION STAGE 7

CHAPTER TWO

I NEED A BREAK

THE SEPARATION STAGE 21

CHAPTER THREE

PLAN YOUR EXIT

THE PREPARATION STAGE 37

CHAPTER FOUR

A LETTER TO SIN

THE EXPLANATION STAGE 51

CHAPTER FIVE

IT'S OVER

THE EXECUTION STAGE 59

CHAPTER SIX

I'M FINALLY FREE

THE FREEDOM STAGE 69

Sylvester Sumler Jr.

Six Reasons it's Hard to Break Up

1. History - The longer you hold on to it, the harder it is to let it go. Over time sin will develop a stronghold in your life.

2. Denial- Often times people don't break up in a relationship because they believe that their relationship is not causing them any harm.

3. Relapse- Many people break up in relationships but return back to the same toxic relationship that they were in. Breaking up with sin can be hard because of the number of times you've failed to let go.

4. Initial Acceptance- Sometimes it's hard to let go of unhealthy relationships when you are attached to the feeling of being wanted and accepted. Sin accepted you at birth and often caters to your natural feelings and desires.

5. Bargaining- Breaking up with sin can be challenging when you bargain with your flesh and accept certain sinful behaviors in your life.

6. Fear of starting over - Breaking up can seem like too much work, and you start to believe that it's better to be comfortable and trapped, than uncomfortable and free. When you are afraid to start over, you won't embrace the challenge of change, because it seems easier to stay where you are.

The Break Up

Chapter One

“I Don't Want to Live Like This” (The Convicting Stage). In this chapter, you must admit that you’ve been in a toxic relationship and acknowledge that there is a better way of living. Realize that you have been living beneath your potential. Before the end of this chapter, you will acknowledge that the sin in your life is not right.

The Break Up

Chapter One

I Don't Want to Live Like This

The Conviction Stage

Have you ever been in a relationship that was damaging to you as a person and a threat to your purpose in life? Maybe, the relationship was distracting you from your schoolwork, causing problems in your business, creating division in your family, or causing you to compromise in your relationship with God.

Perhaps, your relationship looked good on the outside and exemplified the perfect picture of a Power Couple. People admired your relationship and even tried to imitate it.

The only problem is when you found time by yourself, you begin to realize that inside you were unhappy. There was no real connection and you begin to lose your true identity and motivation to achieve your goals.

Maybe you feel exhausted, drained, and unfulfilled. If you're reading this book, you're probably ready for a change and realized that your relationships have been more harmful than helpful. The conviction and tension you feel within has pushed you to a position to finally declare, "I don't want to live like this!"

The Life Jacket

As a Christian, this reminds me of how sin overwhelms us. Like an enormous sea, the distractions of this world can overtake us. I encourage you today, as a starting point, to break away from sin and let the gift of conviction be your life jacket to freedom. The reality is although we have entered a relationship with Jesus Christ there is a constant war between our flesh and the Holy Spirit that lives within us.

This conflict will inspire one to break up with patterns and behaviors that cause damage and ultimately cling to God. There are strongholds, habits, places, people, and acquired lifestyles that we are challenged to break up with. We must act on this process of elimination fervently to reap the benefits of a healthy and whole relationship with Jesus Christ. God doesn't desire to share us with the enemy. God wants our whole heart.

As believers of Jesus Christ, we have been saved from the penalty of sin, nevertheless, we have not been excluded from the presence of sin. Sin presents itself in the form of our human nature, but our spiritual nature in Christ, through the power of the Holy Spirit, should supersede temptation and help us to overcome!

The Warning Light

In an unhealthy relationship, you may have felt something internal that warned you to not proceed. Deep down on the inside, you knew that entering this relationship would hinder you from your purpose. The same internal feeling presents itself in our relationship with Jesus Christ. When you are striving to live a holy and righteous life, there will be moments when you are not defensively strong.

If you are not careful sin will creep in, damage your relationship with God and attempt to make a home in your heart. The blessing in being saved is that salvation comes with many gifts generated by the Holy Spirit. One gift is called conviction, the Christian's warning light.

An indicator that lets the Christian know when they are turning away from God. Our conviction helps us manage our Christian lifestyle and partners with the Holy Spirit in helping us determine what we allow into our hearts and what we should keep out.

When you are disobedient to God, conviction pulls on your conscience and may cause restlessness. That's the Holy Spirit working on the inside to make you better! If you are living outside of God's will, your tolerance level for sin is high.

However, when you profess faith in Jesus Christ, your tolerance level for sin decreases. Your convictions are reflections of your desires, but your will reflects your actions. In other words, you can know something is bad for you and still not be convicted by it. Your convictions are always connected to your passions.

If you are passionate about your relationship with God, your convictions will be strong against sin because sin disconnects you from God. Any serious, passionate, committed Christian should feel something on the inside when they are losing a connection with God. In this case, here are a few important questions for you to raise:

- What convictions do I no longer have?
- What am I comfortable with that I should be uncomfortable with?
- What sin have I allowed to co-exist in my relationship with God?
- Have I packed God up and moved him out of my heart?
- What are my feelings towards God?

Having no convictions is the absence of God in your heart. There is nothing worse than trying to manage an intimate and loving relationship with someone you don't have feelings for! Most

Christians have lost their feelings for God. Some only let God exist in their lives for the sake of convenience without any desire for a real connection. Others only allow God to occupy a little space in their lives until they hit rock bottom and realize they need Him.

To want God means to disown the world. Our

Bible tells us in 1 John 2:15, " Love not the world neither the things that are in the world. If any man loves the world the love of the Father is not in him." Your tolerance level for sin measures your desire to live with God for eternity!

As you start walking with God, you should make a vital decision to live a better life. You should become so fed up, disgusted, and turned off by things that are not of God. If you want to experience deep intimacy with God and long-lasting love for God, your convictions must develop within your dislikes towards sin and become more powerful as your heart for God grows!

In Psalms 51, David cried out to God, “Cast not your presence away from me! Whatever you do, please do not take away my ability to feel your presence!” David also in that same passage says, “against thee have I sinned.” David wanted God to create in him a clean heart and renew a right spirit within him. This passage helps us to understand the power of how to confess our sins and cry out for help when we feel convicted. David's plea of reconciliation shows us how to turn back to God.

The key to keeping your conviction alive in your relationship with Jesus Christ is being in the presence of God. I encourage you to read the passage and stay in God's presence.

The Breakup

The primary key to breaking up with the strongholds of sin in your life is to acknowledge your convictions. Are you a believer in Jesus Christ who no longer feels the way you use to feel in your relationship with God? Are you bound up in the bondage of sin and sinful behaviors? Is your relationship with God infected?

If you answered yes to any of these questions, take a pause from reading this book, place a bookmark on this page, find you a quiet place, and get into the presence of God. Stay there until you feel the chains of sin breaking. Let God capture your heart again.

Regaining a connection with God will lead you towards freedom in Jesus Christ. If you are going to break up with a life of sin you must decide that a life worth living, is a life that is free from the bondage of sin!

The Break Up

A Prayer of Reconciliation

Dear God, Help me to hate the things you hate and want the things you want! Give me your heart's desire and change the way I feel about the sin in my life.

I realize that I am in desperate need of a breakup. I am tired and frustrated with my lifestyle and I want to love You completely and be free from the entrapment of sin. Allow me to feel Your presence and forgive me for holding on to customs, habits, and behaviors that are against Your will.

I surrender my all to You. Deliver me, God. I desire to be free from the stronghold of sin. In the name of Jesus. Amen.

Reference Scriptures:

- ***Psalm 38:18***
- ***John 16:8***
- ***Luke 15:21***
- ***Psalm 51:3***
- ***Psalm 32:3***
- ***Luke 5:8***

The Break Up

Chapter Two

"I Need a Break" (The Separation Stage). In this chapter, you will be challenged to separate yourself by creating as much distance from sin as you can. You will do through fasting, devotion, worship, praying, and meditation.

The Break Up

Chapter Two

I Need A Break

The Separation Stage

Taking a break is never easy. Leaving someone or something that once gave you satisfaction and has been connected to your life is not always easy to disconnect from. There are many signs that occur in relationships that could indicate that it might be time for a break.

This usually happens in a relationship when two people are having a hard time co-existing with each other and agree to separate. As a believer in Jesus Christ, there are certain lifestyles, mindsets, and behaviors that should not be connected to your life. The truth is you simply don't belong together! In fact, just admit it, “You can't stand each other.”

The primary reason you need a break as a follower of Christ is the Spirit of God who lives on the inside of you is in total disagreement with your sinful nature. Therefore, if you do not separate what's not pleasing to the Spirit your relationship with God will fall apart.

The Bible says in 1 John 1:5 that God is light and in Him, there is no darkness. God wants you to walk in His light and not be ruled by the works of darkness. For example, when a couple chooses to take a break from a toxic relationship, they stop all communication and create a substantial amount of distance from each other.

In the same manner, this is the process of breaking up with sin. When sin becomes familiar and has attached a stronghold to your life it disconnects you from the will of God. This reminds me of Joseph when he was approached by Potiphar's wife in Genesis 39. She wanted to have sex with Joseph, but Joseph refused her offer and ran out of the house. If you are going to be free in Jesus, there will be some moments where you will have to take off running. I believe if Joseph would have stayed longer, he might have fallen victim to his flesh and sinned. Just like Joseph, there will be times that you have to break away from the presentation of sin and take off running.

While on a break from your sinful lifestyle, old desires are going to approach you, old habits are going to represent themselves to you, distractions will enter into your life but you must guard your heart and if necessary take off running. The Bible is clear when it tells us to resist the devil and he will flee from you!

If you're wondering what your next step should be in regaining a strong connection with God; This is the perfect time for you to establish a break! It's easy to get accustomed to the feelings of sin. The moments of pleasure and the need to be accepted.

Have you had enough disappointments? Are u willing to take another loss to your flesh? You have allowed yourself to entertain a lifestyle that has delayed your destiny, distanced you from God, and is causing you your greatest pain! Break away now and find victory in Jesus Christ.

He is waiting with open arms to accept you just as you are in the kingdom of God. Your addiction, struggles, and habits will haunt you for the rest of your life. You have the power in Jesus Christ to be free from sin.

Many Christians have attachments to sin that they are not willing to separate from. I believe that many followers of Christ have accepted God's grace in the idea that it will keep them, but not God's grace in the idea that it will change them. Here's the truth, your stronghold of sin is not a thorn in the flesh, it is a threat to your spirit! Pack your bags and make up in your mind to separate yourself from the sins that overtake you.

Get as far away as you can and decide that you are breaking away from the strongholds of sin. Take one day at a time. Breaking away from long term habits, generational curses, and bondages of sin will not be easy. If you are serious about disconnecting from sin and living a life of freedom you will need to make some challenging and uncomfortable decisions.

It is vital that you walk through each day with focus and determination to become free! After two people have decided to distance themselves from an unhealthy relationship, they begin to fill that space with something to keep them occupied. They simply redirect their attention.

For instance, they work out at the gym, join an organization, further their education, discover or perfect an interesting hobby. Simply put, the goal is to focus your attention on something other than your current struggle. When taking a break from sin, the first thing you should do is redirect your attention solely to God. You should discover new ways to be more like the Savior, Jesus Christ. During the break, you should commit to talking to God every day to build a better relationship that is intimate and promising.

Sin is a distraction from God and results in a total disconnection with God. Have you noticed a deficiency in your prayer life? Prayer is an outlet and keeps you in continual communication with God and it gives you the power you need to sustain in moments of weakness.

Prayer connects your desires with God's desires. The more you pray, the less you will desire the things that cater to your flesh. When you take a break, make it a priority to pray. I promise you in the midst of your prayers God will give you guidance and grant you peace like a river.

You will also need a spiritual mentor who is experienced and trustworthy who will pray over you and with you, listen to your concerns and share in your moments of joy and growth. This is ultimately the time to cultivate a best friend relationship with God!

During your breaking away from sin, tell God everything! Like the famous hymn, "What a friend we have in Jesus." tell Jesus how you feel, what you're struggling with, and how your strongholds have caused you to be broken and empty. Take everything to God in prayer. God will answer your prayers and He wants to occupy the space in your heart that you've been giving to your flesh. At this stage, God requires all of your attention.

In order to manage a successful break from sin and the will to maintain your distance, you will need to learn how to maximize your time. Did you know sin and time have a lot in common? Time never stops and neither does sin.

The question becomes, what are you doing with your time? One of my favorite preachers,

Pastor Tolan Morgan often states, "The key to sin management is time management."

His argument is that if you manage your time well and serve the Lord, you won't have time for sin. Good time management will automatically decrease the amount of sin in your life. I'm asking you again, what are you doing with your time?

Sin cannot exist outside of time and when it is presented to you in the form of temptation, it always requires an appointment with time. In order for sin to control your life, there must be availability. When there is availability for sin, there will be an opportunity for sin! Sin always has its best chance at the moment when you have nothing else to do.

During your break from sin, you should take advantage of every second God allows you to breathe. After you have committed to a break, you should increase your service to God! This moment should lead you towards serving the church, volunteering in the community, maximizing the usage of your gifts, increasing your devotion to God, and working on your personal and spiritual development.

There is simply too much to do for you to spend most of your time entertaining sin. As Christians, too often we pray for more power, but we really just need to learn how to master productivity. Christians who are experiencing freedom in Christ are Christians who have productive lives. Your greatest issue with the sin in your life is that you have too much time on your hands!

If you live in purpose and manage your time, you will decrease your availability and vulnerability towards sin! Could it be that you are living beneath your purpose because you are too available for sin? God has amazing plans for your life and if you are going to break away from sin, you have got to take control of your time.

Keep Your Distance

In an unhealthy relationship, when a couple decides to take a break, they commit to keeping their distance to avoid conflict. If you remain too close to the person, you will not be able to make a change because the love you have for the person will sometimes cause you to ignore the problems and remain stuck in your toxic relationship.

If you don't remove yourself from sin, you will remain stuck in bondage. You need to establish the distance to avoid conflict between your flesh and the Holy Spirit. As believers of Jesus Christ, we must understand that the closer we are to God, the further away we are from sin and the more we take on the Holy Spirit.

Every time you commit a sin, it is always connected to a place. Sin has a habitat. In order to change your lifestyle and break away from sin, you must change your environment. Make a commitment today to no longer live in sinful environments. If you have a stronghold with drinking too much alcohol, you shouldn't eat dinner at a bar. Limit any environments that promote alcoholic beverages.

If you have an issue with lust, you shouldn't be searching sites that are promoting sex and you should be controlling what you are watching on television. Wherever your struggle is located you have to remove yourself from the habitat that's connected to your sin.

When sin rings the doorbell of your heart, don’t open the door! If you don’t open the door for sin, the chances of it coming into your heart are very unlikely. Stop driving to their house, stop calling that person who is influencing your sinful relationship, stop spending your money on it at the store, stop hanging out at the same spot, stop allowing company into your bedroom to chill, stop spending your time with just anybody.

Most of the time, we let sin walk through the front door and then pray about it later. Don't give sin a home, change your environment and you will eliminate a lot of the sin in your life.

During this break away from sin, place yourself in spiritual environments and create habitats that will influence your deliverance. Don't set yourself up to lose the battle to sin. Jesus died for your sins, conquered death and gave you the victory! If you want to be free from sin, break away from the place that keeps connecting you to your strongholds. The best place to be is in the presence of God! Examine where you are and place yourself in environments that promote God's presence.

A Prayer for Separation

Dear Heavenly Father, I am in desperate need of a break! Sin has controlled my life for a long time and my desire is to serve you and you alone. I'm asking that you will separate me from everything that is causing me to disconnect from you.

Help me to manage my time and increase my service to you. Give me the discernment that comes from the Holy Spirit so I can make a decision that will lead me toward a pure relationship with you.

Give me the strength to separate from old sinful desires, unhealthy people, and places that promote sin. Stand at the center of my heart and don't allow anything but your righteousness to enter. While on this break of separation, my prayer is that you use me to your glory. Show me my purpose so I might serve your kingdom. I'm available to you Lord!

Make me over, reshape my thinking and increase your presence in my life! I don't ever want to go back to the way I use to live! Take my hand and lead me towards victory over my sin. In the name of the one who has all power over the grave and death, Jesus Christ. Amen.

Reference scriptures

- **2 Timothy 2:22**
- **2 Corinthians 6:17**
- **Romans 12:2**
- **Matthew 6:24**

Chapter Three

"Plan Your Exit" (The Preparation Stage). This chapter will equip your mind with the word and layout a spiritual plan that will lead you towards total freedom. You will utilize the strategy of the scriptures to take the next steps in your journey to spiritual transformation. Sometimes people will stay in relationships longer than they desire, simply because they don't know how to leave.

The Break Up

Chapter Three

Plan your Exit

The Preparation Stage

Breaking up requires you to be committed to the change you want to see in spite of the challenges that come along with letting go. Leaving a toxic relationship would be easy if both individuals wanted to leave and end the relationship.

The challenge is when one person in the relationship wants to leave, but the other person wants to stay, and have not embraced the reality of letting go! You may hear them say things like, "This ain't over" or "I've invested too much into this for our relationship to end like this." You may be faced with more promises of how they are making changes to make the relationship better.

The reality is sometimes letting go doesn't just end because you have the desire to leave!

Breaking up requires strategic effort and a well-developed plan to wiggle out of a dead and unwanted relationship. This is true in your relationship with sin! Just because you are saved and want to live your life in a manner that honors God, doesn't mean that sin is just going to cut ties and allow you to flourish in your developing relationship with Christ.

In fact, the enemy is constantly planning attacks, distractions, trips, and falls designed to keep you in the strongholds of sin. You may want to be free, but the enemy wants you to remain entangled up in a life of sin. If you are going to break up from a life of sin, it's going to require you to take some calculated steps toward your freedom and a plan that will lead you to victory. You will have to plan your exit.

Think for a second, everything worth having requires a plan. If you want to save money, you need a plan. If you want to take a vacation, you need a plan, if you want to remodel your home, you need a plan. If you want to mentor a young teen, you need a plan, if you want to go back to school, you have to follow a plan.

My question would be how are you going to live for Christ and break up with your sinful behaviors if you haven't developed a plan? When you fail to plan in your life, you will often stop the possibility of progress in your life. The problem I see with Christians in our modern-day society is that we are so vulnerable to anything the enemy throws at us, most of us enjoy the presence of God but we never investigate the plans of God that he has given us through his word. Could it be that you have been stuck in sins trap because you never truly examined the map God has set out for you to follow?

I want you to know that there is nothing that you can go through in your life of sin that you can't escape from. The Bible tells us in 1 Corinthians 10:13 that God is faithful and with every temptation, God will provide a way of escape.

This suggests to you that any addiction you are facing, the level of abuse you are experiencing, the pain from previous years of your childhood, the struggle against fornication, the fight against poverty, the battle with lust, the shackles of unforgiveness, the adoption of bad habits, the sickness, the depression, the battle you face constantly in your mind; God has already developed a pathway for you to escape!

Therefore, you can never permanently be trapped by the shackles of sin because God has already given you predetermined directions in his word that are specifically designed for any situation that you may find yourself surrounded in.

Equip Yourself with the Word

In order to plan your exit for breaking up, you need to be certain first of how you are going to leave. Often times when couples have had enough in their current relationship, they will begin planning their exit.

Have you ever been in a relationship and your significant other started rapidly creating unnecessary arguments that seemed to have no substance? Maybe you were dating someone, and they started to become very busy without warning and your quality time spent with them was beginning to decrease.

Did you ever experience a deep unwanted silence and the conversation between you and your partner had become forced? Have you ever considered maybe that was their way of initiating their exit? When strategizing your escape, you have to think ahead when it comes to your flesh. Let's take a look at what the Bible says about breaking up with sin! Your exit plan of being free from sin should be born out of the blueprint of God's word. If you are fighting your flesh with anything other than the word, you are using the wrong weapon.

In preparing to break away from your bondage you must equip yourself with the knowledge of God! It is important that you understand that because God is sovereign, his intended plan for our lives is without error. The question I want to ask you is why won't you use God's perfect plan in his word to guide you into freedom?

One reason you are losing the battle against your flesh is not that you lack strength. Your failure to overcome your struggle is because of your lack of knowledge. For example, think about the sin you continue to submit to, the addiction that has you shackled, the brokenness that captured your heart; would you be able to tell me the scriptures in the Bible that speak to your current struggle? The truth is that the stronghold of sin that controls your life will never be lifted automatically. You will have to use the word of God to break away from sin's submission.

Many Christians in response to their sin and struggles stop their efforts at prayer but never make it to dissecting and personalizing the word of God for their situation. You must understand that your prayers are directed towards God, but the word of God is directed towards you! The Bible is not for God; He is the word! The word of God is for you!

The Bible is tailored to fit any trial or struggle you may face. The Bible is your blueprint for your life and contains power that will assist you with your greatest struggles against sin. The Bible tells you what to do when to do it, and how to do it? God never meant for us to go through life trying to figure it out, he left us a comforter the holy spirit and the Bible which contains his plan for our lives!

The answers you been searching for, the power you have been praying for, The freedom you have been waiting for is found in the Word of God!

The Blueprint to Freedom

Exit plan for Depression

Philippians 4:8 "Finally, brethren, whatsoever things are true, whatsoever things are honest, whatsoever things are just, whatsoever things are pure, whatsoever things are lovely, whatsoever things are of good report; if there be any virtue, and if there be any praise, think on these things."

Exit plan for Adultery

Hebrews 13:4 "Marriage should be honored by all, and the marriage bed kept pure, for God will judge the adulterer and all the sexually immoral."

Exit plan for Lust

Galatians 5:16 "So I say, walk by the Spirit, and you will not gratify the desires of the flesh."

Exit plan for Fear

2 Timothy 1:7 "For God hath not given us the spirit of fear, but of power, and of love, and of a sound mind."

Exit plan for Fornication

1 Corinthians 7:2 "But since sexual immorality is occurring, each man should have sexual relations with his own wife, and each woman with her own husband."

Exit plan for Low self-esteem

1 Peter 2:9 "But ye are a chosen generation, a royal priesthood, a holy nation, a peculiar people;

that ye should shew forth the praises of him who hath called you out of darkness into his marvelous light."

Exit plan for Unforgiveness

Mark 11:25 "And when ye stand praying, forgive, if ye have ought against any: that your Father also which is in heaven may forgive you your trespasses."

Exit plan for stress

Philippians 4:6-7 "Be careful for nothing, but in everything by prayer and supplication with thanksgiving let your requests be made known unto God. And the peace of God, which passeth all understanding, shall keep your hearts and minds through Christ Jesus."

Exit plan for sickness

Isaiah 53:5 "But he was wounded for our transgressions, he was bruised for our iniquities: the chastisement of our peace was upon him, and with his stripes, we are healed."

A Prayer for an Exit

Dear Lord, My heart longs to be free but It seems like my sin has trapped me for so long, that I don't know which steps to take toward my freedom. I need you father to show me the strategies of your word so that I may apply it to my daily life! Fill me with your principles and give me the wisdom to break free from every chain in my life! Fill me with your word so that my steps will be ordered by your will. Lord show me an exit so that I may live in the liberty and abundance of life in you. In Jesus name Amen!

The Break Up

Chapter Four

"A Letter to Sin" (The Explanation Stage). In order to move forward, every relationship will need some form of closure. This chapter presents a letter breaking up with sin and a prayer for a transformed mind.

The Break Up

Chapter Four

A Letter to Sin

The Explanation Stage

Whenever a couple decides to break up, there will often be an explanation attached to their decision. There are many reasons people decide to depart from each other.

Some couples split up because they've been involved in an abusive relationship. Another factor people leave each other is because infidelity is involved. There are also people that depart solely when they find that they are no longer compatible and have conflicting aspirations and expectations for life.

Breaking up with your relationship with sin has an explanation of why your spirit can no longer entertain a life of sin. I want to be clear because the issue in your relationship with sin has less to do with what sin has done to you, but it's about what God has done in you. In fact, I wrote this letter to sin, explaining our break up.

Dear sin,

What I'm about to say will not be easy for you to understand but because you have been a consistent part of my life, I want to offer an explanation of why we are breaking up. I understand that you are a part of my nature, but you will no longer be part of my normal. You have shaped my thoughts and lifestyle, causing me to journey on a road to destruction.

My relationship with God had become a routine because of my devotion to my fleshly desires. Serving others was no longer a passion because sin activated my selfish nature. My worship to God was becoming dry and my faith was being infected by the disease of sin.

My peace was attacked because God was getting a piece of my heart, while I was sharing the other piece with the enemy. I wasted so much time and I've missed so many Christ opportunities.

The time I could have been sowing seeds, I was sinning. The times I should have been praying, I was partying. When I could have been living in purpose, I was drowning in my pain. You hurt me spiritually and physically. My family suffered from my addiction. You caused my purpose to be delayed and my productivity to decrease. My appearance changed and I was sinking deep in sin and for a while, I thought I would never be able to start over.

Although you have caused so much damage to my life, The motivation for writing this letter to you derives not only from what sin has done to me but what God is doing inside of me. I'm not sure if you noticed but I'm not the same person today as when we first met. A lot about me has changed.

The biggest change is my desire to please the Lord. My ambitions are directed towards Jesus Christ and how I can become successful in the kingdom of God! There is nothing I am more excited about then building my faith and living as an ambassador for Christ. The lifestyle that use to bring me fulfillment, now makes me feel empty.

Every day I am chasing after God's presence and aiming to live a lifestyle that reflects God's heart. I also have a new focus and a new purpose. There are people who are waiting on me to be free so that I can minister to them! Being a slave to sin blinded my focus and kept me focused on everything but my walk with the Lord.

Now that I realize that the enemy has no control over me; I am choosing to no longer entertain any old mindsets, habits, or addictions that I have experienced. I'm just not interested anymore! There is more God has for me to experience in him but if I don't break away from you now, I will remain stuck in slavery to my flesh. God wants to take me and show me the promised land! This relationship has gone on longer than it should have but today I declare it's over. One thing I have learned in this toxic relationship is that no matter how much wrong I've done; God has provided me grace for every time I've let him down!

This relationship of sin helped me understand God's love and how my sin didn't stop him from loving me, but my sin revealed the expression of God's love for me. If Jesus Christ can die for me than surely, I can live for him. I hope you get this letter because this is the last time, I'll be in conversation with you, my time will be spent walking in the freedom and deliverance that Jesus Christ has given me. The psalmist says, "I am free praise the Lord I am free, no longer bound, no more chains holding me!"

Sincerely,

A Transformed Mind

Prayer,

Dear Lord, thank you for giving me the closure I needed and for opening my eyes to see that you have better in store for me than what I've currently experienced. Thank you that you didn't run out of patience, but you are constantly leading me toward a fruitful and favorable life in you! I give you my heart and I commit myself to your will. Guide me toward freedom and I believe by faith that the victory is mine and the battle is already won! In Jesus name, Amen.

Chapter Five

“It's Over” (The Execution Stage). Face it, stand up to it, walk it out. In this chapter, you will be faced with the fight for your life. You will face your current struggles and fight your way to freedom. This will be the hardest stage on your journey to spiritual transformation, but you must keep fighting.

The Break Up

Chapter Five

It's Over

The Execution Stage

One of the most common actions that occur when couples break up is that couples usually get back together a few times before the break up is final. When you've been in a relationship with someone for a long period of time it is quite natural for couples to find an excuse why the two shouldn't break up. As excuses arise it prolongs the break up and makes it even harder to let go.

The best thing you can do when breaking up from a toxic relationship is staying committed to your decision to be free. This is true with our spiritual bondage, if your desire is to break up with the sin in your life it will require you to be committed to becoming free. When you declare that it's over, let it be over.

This will require your will to be strong and your mind to be committed to what you declared out of your mouth. The question becomes, How do you stay committed to breaking up with the sin in your life?

First, you need an accountability partner. There has to be somebody that you intentionally put in place that will hold you accountable for your actions. Let me be honest, the struggle you are facing in your life, you will not be able to execute and navigate toward victory on your own. In this stage, you will have to become extremely honest with yourself and your accountability partner.

Share your boundaries, your weaknesses, and the specifics of what you are struggling with. Next, you need affirmation. You have to constantly speak victory over your life daily. This reminds you of where you are headed, who you are, and helps you maintain your focus of being free. There is power in the tongue.

In fact, the Bible declares that life and death are in the power of the tongue. What you say is directly associated with how you will live! Your words have power and your destiny can often be directed by what you declare out of your mouth! If you are going to execute your victory you have to let victory come out of your mouth.

Also, in order to execute the break up you have to live out your assignment on the earth. God gives every believer an assignment. Don't spend time bargaining with your flesh. Go after your assignment. Living out your assignment or calling helps you to remain in alignment with God. When you are living out your assignment it assists you in the fight with sin because it's harder for the enemy to get to you when you are operating in the place and purpose God has called you to operate in.

Fight off Sinful Urges

You must understand the fight that is attacking your life! This is not a wrestling match or a boxing match. This fight of the flesh is not physical it's spiritual.

Therefore, you cannot use physical tactics or human reasoning, you must be guided and led by the spirit. James 4:7 tells us to submit yourselves to God, resist the devil and he will flee from you.

This fight will not be easy. This fight will call for much resistance, many scars, and the willingness to deny your flesh. There will be days in which you will want to quit and revert back to your struggle with sin. The truth is that the fight of breaking free from your addiction will not end in a knockout. You will have to fight your way through every round.

The quicker your spirit responds to your flesh the easier the fight. When fighting sin, you will have some moments when you feel strong but don't let your guard down, the temptation of sin will come back again to test you. Jesus was tempted three times on the mountain in Matthew Chapter 4 before the devil backed off.

Notice how Jesus fought him. He didn't use his fist, but he uses the word of God. You must be war-ready in the spirit at all times. Sin will sneak up on you without you knowing its presence because sin always attacks you where you are vulnerable and weak. You can win the fight by using the word, that will be your only weapon in overcoming your flesh.

When fighting against the temptation of sin, the word of God should be at the top of your mind and at the tip of your tongue. When fighting through your struggles, on your quest toward spiritual freedom it is important that you never look back. When the devil cannot capture you in your present, he will use your past against you, attempting to make you go back towards bondage. It's not that believers don't experience freedom; the problem is once you become free, the tendency to turn back around and revert back to the addiction of sin becomes tempting.

Remember as you journey towards your freedom, it will always be easy to look back when you are not looking up to God. If you knew all of the things God had in mind for your future, you would fight with everything that's in you. You have to make up in your mind no matter how hard the fight to freedom gets, turning back toward your relationship with sin is not an option. You must stay committed to your decision to be free and fight through your flesh until you reach total freedom in your life!

A Prayer for New Commitment

Dear Lord, help me to stay committed to the break up with the sin in my life! Show me an accountability partner that I can lean on in times of weakness. Give me the strength to fight to the end and allow me to never revert back to my past. Give me the strategies to execute your word in my life that I may not sin against your will. I declare that I am looking forward and I declare right now that I'm walking into total victory over sin! In Jesus name, Amen.

Reference scriptures

- **James 4:7**
- **Romans 6:14**
- **John 10:10**
- **1John1:7**

The Break Up

Chapter Six

“I'm Finally Free” (The Freedom Stage). In this chapter, you are living in purpose, and the chains are no longer holding you down. At this stage, you are experiencing total freedom and the victory over sin has been won.

The Break Up

Chapter Six

I'm Finally Free

The Freedom Stage

Whenever you break up from a toxic relationship with a significant other, you will gain the peace that you haven't felt in a long time. There is a release that takes place in your mind and spirit that empowers you to walk into a new level of strength.

The reality is when you finally become free everything inside of you will sense your new freedom. True freedom will ease the pain of your past and direct the posture of your heart towards thanksgiving. During this stage, there will be much rejoicing because you have taken the devil's best shot and through Jesus Christ, you have overcome the bondage of sin. You are experiencing freedom today because you didn't accept your bondage.

Freedom is yours because you committed yourself to God and submitted to the process of spiritual transformation.

Can you believe it? You never thought you would be at this stage of finally being free, but you made it. Now that you are free, what is next?

Embrace New Possibilities

Sin no longer has control over you and new possibilities are awaiting you. Being a slave to sin has caused you to live beneath your potential, but now that you're free the possibility of what you can become is limitless.

The break up of sin in your life has given you more time to explore new opportunities, new passions, new dreams, and new altitudes! Can you sense it? I am certain that you didn't realize how much space sin was taking in your life! Your time is now to explore a new direction and embrace a new journey in your faith.

The Bible says in II Corinthians 5:17 says, "if any man be in Christ; he is a new creature; old things are passed away; behold all things are become new." This means because Christ is in you and you are in Christ, you are not the same person that you were on yesterday. You are a new person with a new purpose. You are walking with the personality and power of Christ working in your life.

You must understand that there will be some people who will try to attach your past to your current progress in God. You must remember, no matter what you have done, God never identifies you by your past, but he sees you by the potential in which he created you to be. The gift of being free in Christ is that every day you get to walk through the door of new possibilities. It is possible that you may preach the gospel. You may become an advocate for the homeless. God may call you to mentor youth in low-income neighborhoods.

Maybe you will start a non-profit for abused women. I don't know what your next level may consist of, but don't limit your possibility of doing something greater. The fact is sin limited your options and hid your capability. Freedom does the opposite; freedom illuminates your possibility!

The Bible declares in Ephesians 3:20 that "God is able to do exceedingly abundantly above all that we ask or think, according to the power that worketh in us." Now that you are free in Christ the possibility of what you can become is beyond what you can imagine. Freedom in Christ will lead to new and limitless possibilities.

Soar Into Your Destiny

God didn't lead you into spiritual freedom for you to be stagnant, but it is his desire that you soar into your destiny! There is something that God has given you that the world needs to experience. Sin made you settle, but freedom will unleash the opportunity for you to soar! There are gifts, dreams, and talents that have been dormant in your life! When sin gets you, it grabs everything that's connected to you. Now that you are free, there is nothing holding you down! The weight has been lifted and your wings have been repaired! Walk by faith and live without any fear of failure!

When you consider all, you have been through while trapped in bondage, now is the time for you to live your life in confidence and boldness. Your pain wasn't your purpose, but it became a vehicle that led you to your purpose in Christ! This stage of freedom requires you to stretch your faith, reach for your dreams, jump out of your comfort zone, and pursue your destiny with passion and zeal.

Share Your Story

God didn't deliver you so that you could be silent. In fact, the evidence that you are living in freedom is determined by the way you share your story. The bible says in Revelation 12:11 that "they overcame by the blood of the lamb, and by the word of their testimony." This means that freedom is not just for you, but when you receive freedom in Christ you should share your story so that somebody else can receive freedom in their life. Freedom should not lead you into isolation. Freedom should lead you towards community.

The reality is someone is going through the same thing you had to overcome, and your story could give people the strategy and the wisdom needed to overcome their struggle with sin. Freedom gives you a voice. Most Christians who are captured in spiritual bondage suffer alone and in secret. The joy of being free is that you don't have to hide anymore.

There's no longer a need to feel ashamed because of your addiction. Freedom not only gives you a voice, but it increases your volume! You have overcome the worst struggle in your life and the test you overcame left you with a liberating testimony. In the final step to your freedom, you have to find a way to share your story. When you release your story it not only motivates victory for someone else, but it completes your deliverance.

The truth is now that you are totally free, when you tell your story it reminds you of where God has brought you from, and what it took for you to make it to where you are now in God! When you are truly saved from sin, you won't mind sharing your experience with others, because sharing doesn't just save others, sharing continues to save you!

The Break Up

A Prayer of Freedom

Dear God, it feels good to finally be free! Thank you for delivering me from the hand of the enemy. Thank you for giving me the strength to break free of my addiction. Thank you that I didn't die in my disobedience, but your grace was sufficient for me. Your presence kept me while I was in my sin. Your power pulled me out of my sin. Your grace is currently keeping me away from sin. I can say with great assurance that I have the victory! I will spend the rest of my life in effort to live by your word and follow after your will. In Jesus name, Amen.

Reference scriptures

- **Ephesians 3:12**
- **Romans 6:22**
- **1 Peter 2:16**
- **Isaiah 61:1**

Made in the USA
Middletown, DE
14 July 2024

57293469R00051